Transition Attack: 5 Out Transition

Martin Gross

Foreword

As I sit down to pen these words, I can't help but reflect on the journey that has brought me to this moment. For over two decades, I have had the privilege of knowing Marty Gross not just as a colleague, but as a friend. Our shared passion for basketball has bound us together through victories and defeats, through highs and lows of coaching, and through countless hours of strategizing and dreaming.

During our year of coaching together, I had the opportunity to witness firsthand Marty's dedication, knowledge of the game, and relentless pursuit of excellence. But beyond the technical and strategic x and o's what truly sets him apart is his unwavering commitment to his players and the coaches he worked with. He doesn't just teach the game, he instills in them a sense of purpose, resilience, and teamwork that extends beyond the basketball court.

In "Transition Attack: 5 Out Transition", Marty simplifies in a systematic progression how to teach 5 Out Transition. I encourage you to study "the what" and "how" of 5 Out Transition. This book will be an invaluable tool from a seasoned college basketball coach who has coached for 46 years.

Whether you are a seasoned coach looking to refine your strategies or a player aspiring to take your game to the next level, "Transition Attack" should become an invaluable resource in your journey.

I have coached with 2 of Marty's mentors, Greg Walcavich and Willis Wilson so I have seen his evolution as a coach and person over the years and have no doubt this book will leave an indelible mark on all who read it.

Here is your next chapter in your coaching journey. May it be filled with success, growth, and endless opportunities to help others.

With Warm Regards,
Kevin Reynolds
Head Coach
Point Park University

Kevin Reynolds at Point Park University 2022-2024:

- Reynolds led Point Park University to 30 wins and its winningest season ever during the 2023-2024 season.
- First win in the National NAIA Tournament and lost to eventual champion Freed Hardeman in Region final.
- Led Point Park to its first conference postseason title in 23 years.
- Led Point Park to a 53-10 record in the first 2 seasons.
- Led the country in offensive rebounding with 15.8 rebounds per game.
- Led the country in defensive rebounding with 33.0 rebounds per game.
- Led the country in rebound margin with +13 rebounds per game.
- Finished #2 in the country in blocked shots per game with 5.4.

Before Point Park, Reynolds led one of the biggest turnarounds in NCAA Division II in his 10 years at Slippery Rock from 2008-18:

- Reynolds led The Rock to three NCAA Tournament appearances and six 20-win seasons.
- The Rock had single-digit wins in 13 of the previous 14 years before Reynolds' arrival. Reynolds turned things around with an average of 18.8 wins per season in his tenure.
- The 188 wins in 10 years at Slippery Rock were an increase of 112 wins from the previous 10-year period before he arrived. That was the fifth-biggest turnaround in all of NCAA Division II Men's Basketball during that time.
- In over 100 years of Slippery Rock basketball, there have been nine seasons of 20 or more wins. Reynolds engineered six of those.
- Slippery Rock made the NCAA Tournament in Reynolds' third season of 2010-11. The Rock made nationals again in 2012-13 and 2014-15. In the last two of those appearances, Slippery Rock advanced to the second round.
- Reynolds coached and recruited 17 All-PSAC selections in his 10 years at Slippery Rock. There were also seven All-Atlantic Region selections and three NCAA Division II All-Americans.
- Reynolds had 56 student-athletes and/or managers earn undergraduate degrees and 16 earn graduate degrees during his Slippery Rock tenure.
- 18 players signed professional basketball contracts.

Reynolds got his start in coaching as an assistant at Indiana University of Pennsylvania from 1991-95 with some very successful teams under Kurt Kanaskie. He was a part of IUP's rise to national prominence with Elite 8 and Final Four appearances and a record of 56-5 from 1993-95.

Acknowledgment

I want to express my deepest gratitude and sincere appreciation to Ross Comerford and Fast Model Sports for allowing me to use their product, Fast Draw, for this book project. We have used Fast Model products since its beginning in 2004. Fast Draw, Fast Scout, and Fast Recruit have been invaluable tools to the basketball community over the years.

The dedication and commitment demonstrated by Fast Model Sports in developing cutting-edge software technologies tailored specifically for basketball have truly revolutionized the way the sport is analyzed, coached, and appreciated. From enhancing the effectiveness of scouting with Fast Scout or player evaluation processes with Fast Recruit as well as navigating the transfer portal effectively, Fast Model Sports has been at the top of the industry.

Fast Draw has been an integral part of coaching staffs across America to build detailed opponent playbooks, self-study, and game strategic insights. In all, Fast Model Sports has greatly contributed to the overall advancement of basketball.

Table of Contents

Foreword.. i

Acknowledgment iv

Transition Attack_Introduction... 1

Chapter 1

Transition Attack_5 Out Transition_Strengths and Weaknesses.......... 7

Chapter 2

Transition Attack_Screen in Semi-Transition 10

Chapter 3

5 Out Transition_Pass and Follow 13

Chapter 4

5 Out Transition_Elbow Over the Top 15

Chapter 5

5 Out Transition_Elbow Screen Away with DHO (Dribble Handoff)
.... 19

Chapter 6

5 Out Transition_Elbow Split with DHO 24

Chapter 7

5 Out Transition_Play the Weakside Exchange........................... 29

Chapter 8

5 Out Transition_Reject Screen Away... 31

Chapter 9

5 Out Transition_Screen Away and Roll....................................... 33

Chapter 10

5 Out Transition_Screen Re-Screen.. 35

Chapter 11

5 Out Transition_Stagger to Horns Dribble at Backdoor 38

Chapter 12

5 Out Transition_Stagger-On Ball-Cut the Help 41

Chapter 13

5 Out Transition_Reverse of Ball Denied-Play the Other Way 44

Glossary 54

About The Author 71

Transition Attack
Introduction

When I coached at Wichita State University from 2007-2011, we made a conscious effort to run after makes and misses in year two. This was a dramatic change for us because our system was predicated on running only after missed field goals and walking the ball up after a made field goal.

We had a complicated system in place of sequencing plays three plays at a time. We would add or subtract sets during deadball situations. So, the conversation was not a simple change philosophically for us. Our head coach at the time, Gregg Marshall, had a belief that your team's defense would suffer if the decision was made to run after both makes and misses.

At the same time, we knew by running after made baskets we could add 5-7 seconds for our motion or quick hits. In addition, the defense was less likely to be set. Running can create converting advantages. The third consideration for us was we were more talented and athletic in our second year vs. our first year at WSU.

Simply, transition offense begins any time the ball changes hands either by a basket, turnover, or defensive rebound. How fast that transition is depends on your philosophy and how fast you want to play.

Areas of the court defined:

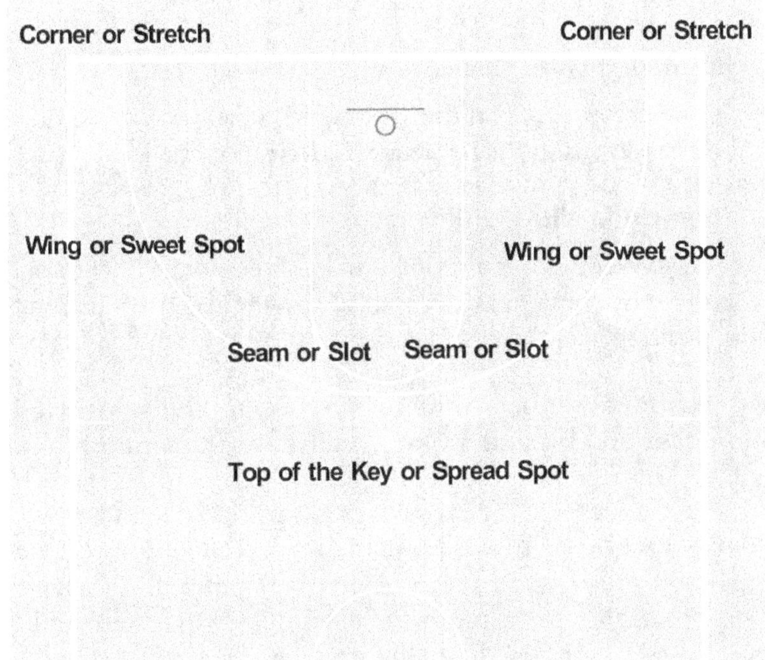

Key characteristics of a transition attack in basketball include:

1. **Speed:**

   Teams aim to advance the ball up the court as quickly as possible to catch the opposing defense off-guard.

2. **Fast Breaks:**

One common element of a transition attack is the fast break, where players sprint down the court to take advantage of numerical or positional mismatches.

3. **Ball Movement:**

Good ball movement and passing are crucial to creating open shots and scoring opportunities in transition.

4. **Decision-Making:**

Players need to make quick decisions on whether to pass, shoot, or drive to the basket based on the situation.

5. **Capitalizing on Chaos:**

Transition attacks thrive on creating chaos and exploiting any breakdowns in the opposing defense.

6. **Transition Three-Pointers:**

In some cases, teams look to take three-point shots during the transition attack to capitalize on the defense being out of position.

Let's also define the difference between drags, quick hits, motion, fast breaks, and 5 Out because we transition into all of these.

1. Primary Fast Break is transition resulting in 1 on 0, 2 on 1, 3 on 1, 3 on 2, or essentially when the offense has "numbers" to attack and pressure the rim after a turnover, rebound, or long rebound. The offense should score on these opportunities 95% of the time if not more.

2. A drag is a screen in transition or semi-transition by a trailing player, usually a big, but not necessarily a big, followed by some offensive action to attack or pressure the rim. Golden State likes to set guard-

on-guard drag screens in semi-transition to free up Curry or Thompson. A diagram shows this in Chapter 2.

3. A quick hit in transition is a set or play that can be executed when the trail post or ballhandler arrives. Some like to call this a "secondary break".

4. Transitioning into your team's motion is also popular. Instead of starting motion from a stack set or another formation, teams "flow" into their half-court motion.

5. The 5-out motion offense is an alternative approach to transition and primary offense for basketball teams at any level, but especially youth basketball teams. It's a position-less offense that relies on spacing the floor and a set of rules that assists players in determining their movements and actions. Essentially, it is a read-and-react offense.

Transition Attack Questions and Thoughts:

1. If you are going to run after makes and misses, you must be **_committed_** to the "run game"!

2. The question that must be asked before deciding to run is, "What can we as a team and coaching staff live with?"

3. Can you live with more turnovers, because teams that run typically average more turnovers per game than teams that do not?

4. Can you live with more bad shots, because as hard as you teach good shot, bad shot, time, and score; your team will take more bad shots than teams that play possession by possession.

5. There is a prevailing theory that teams that are committed to running suffer at the defensive end. I am not sure I agree with this, but if it is true, can you live with a porous defense at times?

6. The decision will have to be made about who takes the ball out after a made basket or can you live with the 4 and 5 taking the ball out?

7. Can you commit to allowing a 2-man or 3-man to advance the ball in transition or bringing a postman back to help, if the point guard gets "jammed" on the outlet pass?

8. How many "secondary breaks" will you run into?

9. How many to too many? Not enough? When Roy Williams coached at North Carolina, for instance, they ran into about a dozen "quick hits" or their motion.

10. Are you willing to commit a substantial amount of practice time to the "run game" including Offense-Defense-Offense segments?

11. If you have the question, "Can we still run sets and incorporate a "run game", watch Michigan State play. Few teams push the ball harder or faster. They run sets to sets or sets to ball screen action after their initial push and it has worked for them for years.

12. Should we consider running more because our fan base wants us to play faster? Fans don't always understand what goes into the "run game". In addition, if turnovers are more prevalent the faster your team plays, running can look ugly.

13. Should we run more because our players want to run more? It sounds sexy, but at the end of the day, it is not easy, and like anything else a commitment must be made to coach, teach, and drill daily, especially the pace at which you want to play to be effective.

14. Does an aggressive mindset to run lead to an aggressive mindset to rebound defensively so that the team can get out and run?

15. Will teams rebound offensively less aggressively and devote fewer players to the offensive boards if they know a team relies heavily on transition scores?

16. Does an up-tempo team favor a well-conditioned team?

17. Does getting the ball out of the net, inbounds, and up the floor beat press defenses?

18. As a coach will you use more players or fewer players if you decide to run? Do you have the personnel to run?

All this being said, in April 2020, Jordan Sperber wrote an article for Hoop Vision. His data helps reinforce the inherent benefits of a transition push.

Since the 2010 season:

- The average points per *transition* play is 1.04
- The average points per *half-court* play is 0.87

Everybody's team is different and unique. As a head coach or an assistant coach part of a staff, you must make the decision best for your team.

Chapter 1
Transition Attack 5 Out Transition
Strengths and Weaknesses

The 5-out motion offense is an alternative approach to transition and primary offense for basketball teams at any level, but especially youth basketball. It's a position-less offense that relies on spacing the floor. There is a set of rules that assist players in reading the defense, reacting to the defense, and determining the smartest cut.

5 Out Strengths:

1. 5 Out Motion creates position-less players – All 5 players on the court are required to pass, cut, dribble, shoot, and screen. This is especially important in youth basketball but also is advantageous at higher levels.

2. Players learn how to play basketball in 5 Out Motion. This is an important benefit no matter the level. Players learn to read the defense, react to their teammates and defenders, and make decisions accordingly. This is important to the development of young players, but also more veteran players as well.

3. Every player is involved in 5 Out Motion. All players will be involved and must contribute to the team's offense. One or two players can't dominate the basketball.

4. 5 Out Motion requires great spacing. If players are all in the correct spots on the floor, your team will always have great spacing. Good spacing will create driving lanes which will put the defense in constant rotation or help.

5. 5 Out Motion is difficult for opposing teams to scout. There are many actions, but no sets. Opponents will have to prepare

by defending various actions as opposed to set plays. Since the offensive players learn to read the defense and cut accordingly, it will be hard to defend.

6. Opponents will not be able to defend with a heavy shift to the lane. Defenders will be required to guard all areas of the floor. In addition, because of 5 Out spacing, opponents' post players will have to play away from the basket where they are less comfortable.

7. 5 Out Motion can be used as a delay game. This is especially good if your league doesn't have a shot clock and you want to hold the ball. 5 Out Motion will provide movement and keep the defense honest while giving the appearance of the offense trying to score.

8. 5 Out Motion is easy to teach. One of the best things about the 5 Out Motion is it can be taught systematically in progressions. Coaches can teach as many or few actions depending on their team's basketball IQ. In addition, these actions can be added gradually as the season goes on if necessary.

5 Out Weaknesses:

1. 5 Out Motion is not great if you have a dominant player or two. Everyone is involved including your weaker players.

2. In 5 Out Motion, if you have a dominant low post player, and this includes perimeter players, he will be playing away from the basket and therefore away from his strength.

3. If you play with a shot clock, players tend to play fast, get sped up, and force the action. This can result in misreading the defense and hurried or forced shots at the end of the shot clock result.

4. 5 Out Motion takes time for players to learn the actions and learn how to read and react to the defense. If errors are to be made, error on the side of aggression. Sometimes a player will read the defense incorrectly, but if the offensive player makes a hard, aggressive, scoring cut, he may just be open anyway.

5. In 5 Out Motion, players can get predictable in their cuts almost like robots, especially when they are first learning the movements or actions. When this happens, scoring opportunities are missed.

Chapter 2
Transition Attack
Screen in Semi-Transition

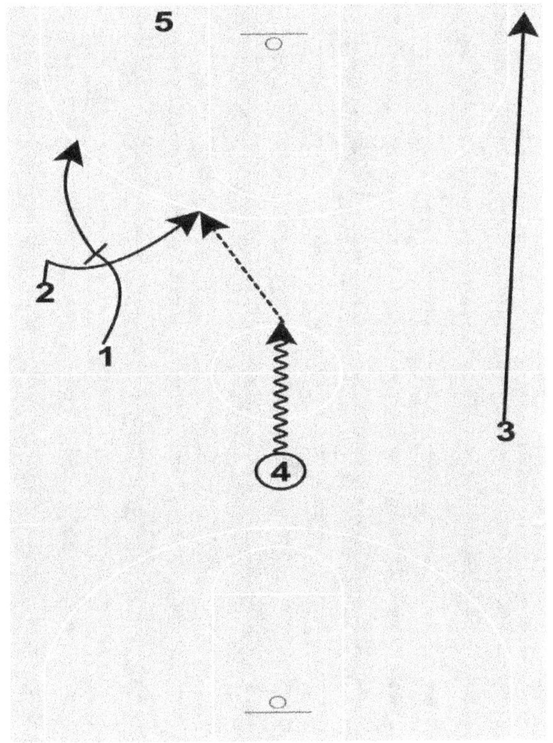

Diagram 1:

4 advances the ball.

5 sprints to the dunk spot or alley.

2 and 3 run the same outer third of the floor.

1/2 brush screen.

4-2 pass.

Screen in Semi-Transition

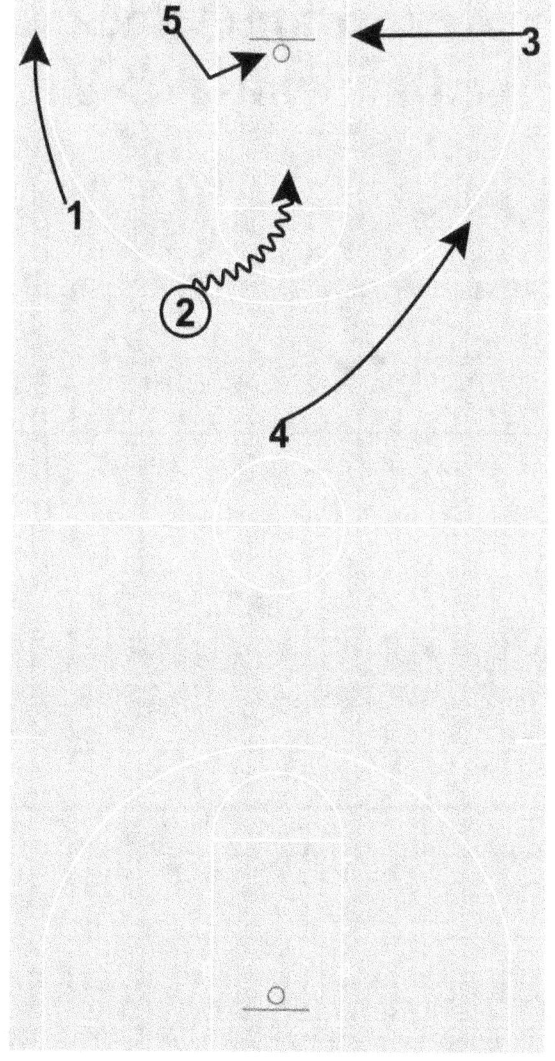

Diagram 2:

1 runs the arc.

4 runs the arc.

3 cuts the help.

5 looks for the lob.

2 makes a play.

Note:

If you have a 4 man who can advance the ball, consider screening in semi-transition.

Golden State likes this action.

Note:

The coach can designate who cuts the help between 4 and 3. Whoever is the better shooter runs the arc.

Chapter 3
5 Out Transition
Pass and Follow

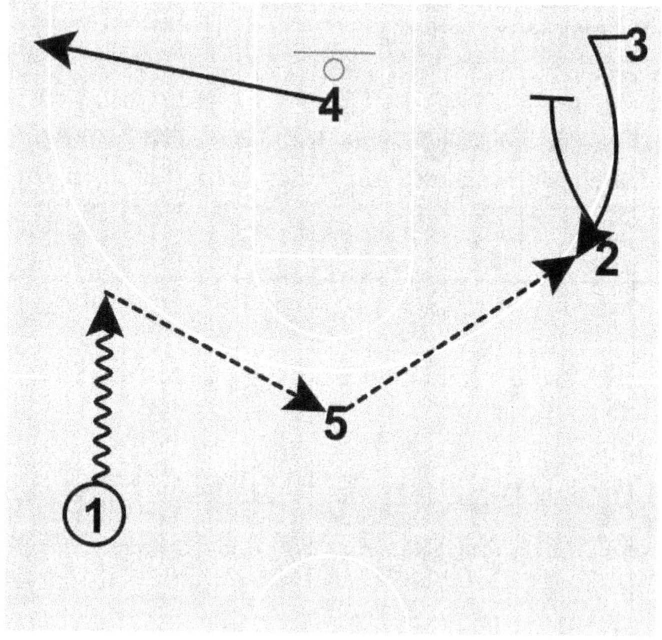

Diagram 1:

4 pressures rim and then releases to the open corner if no pass.

1-5 pass.

2/3 down screen.

5-2 pass.

5 Out Transition
Pass and Follow

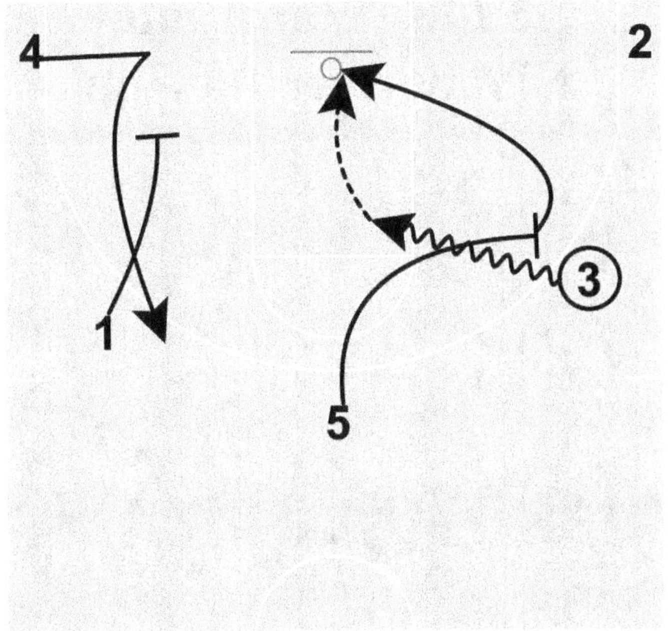

Diagram 2:

1/4 down screen.

5/3 SOB (Screen on Ball).

3 drives to make a play.

5 rolls to score.

3-5 pass for score if open.

Chapter 4
5 Out Transition
Elbow Over the Top

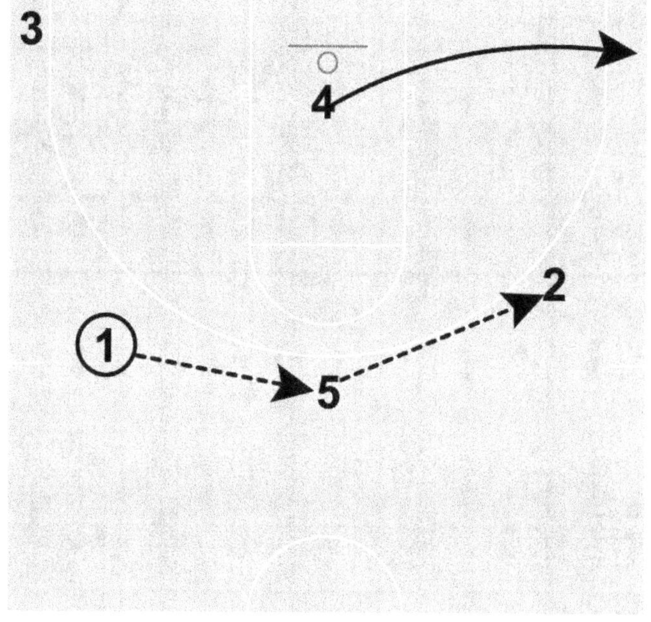

Diagram 1:

4 rim runs and clears to the open corner if no pass.

1-5-2 reverse of the ball.

5 Out Transition
Elbow Over the Top

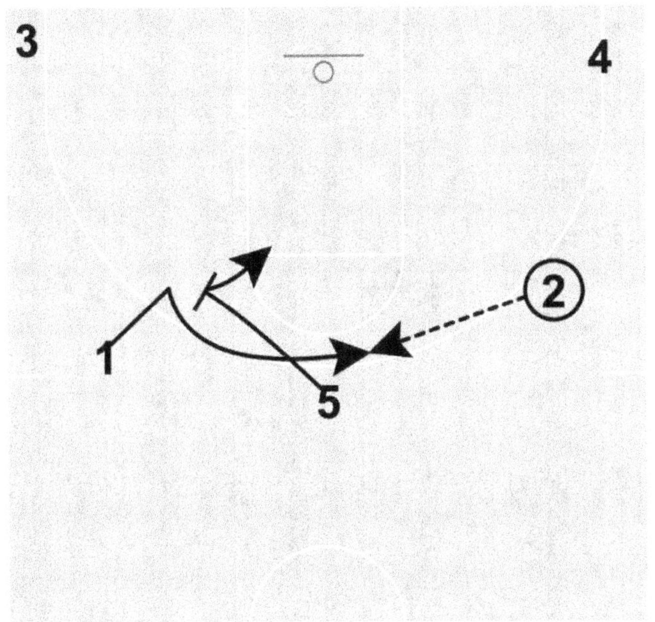

Diagram 2:

5/1 down screen.

2-1 pass.

5 spaces to the weak elbow.

5 Out Transition
Elbow Over the Top

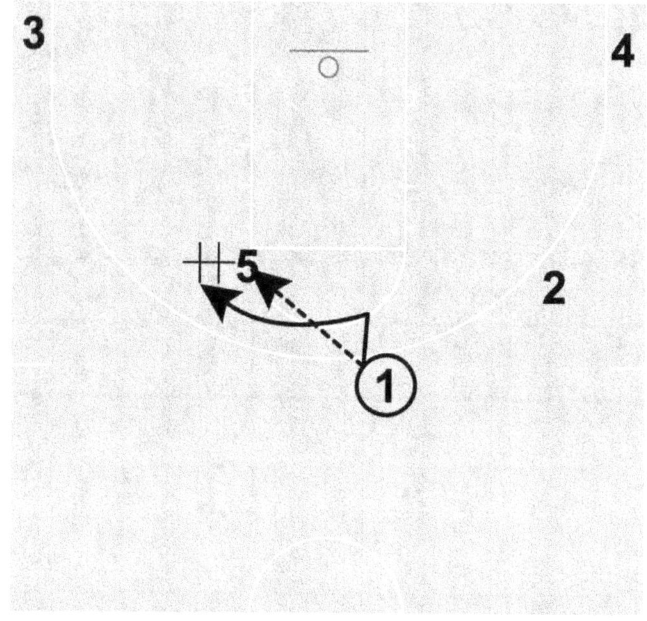

Diagram 3:

1-5 pass pinch post.

1 cuts over the top of 5.

5-1 HO (Handoff)

5 Out Transition
Elbow Over the Top

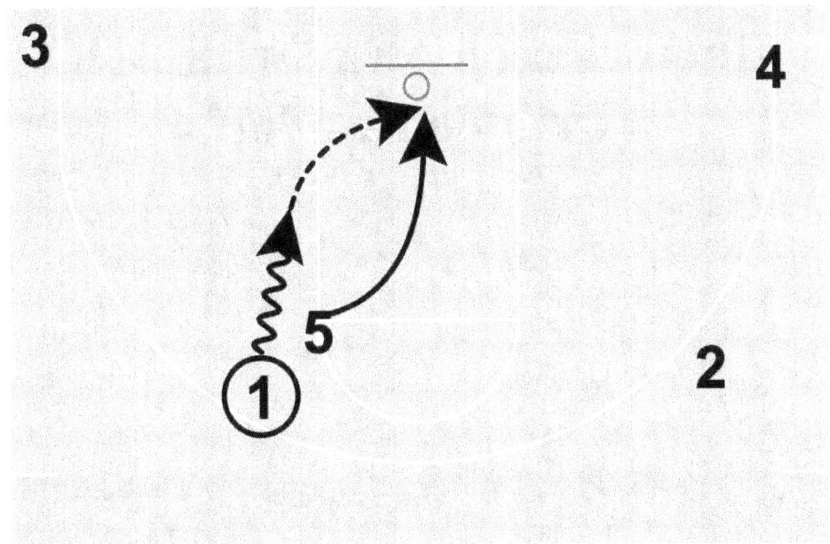

Diagram 4:

1 drives to make a play.

5 rolls to score.

1-5 pass for score if open.

Chapter 5
5 Out Transition
Elbow Screen Away with DHO
(Dribble Handoff)

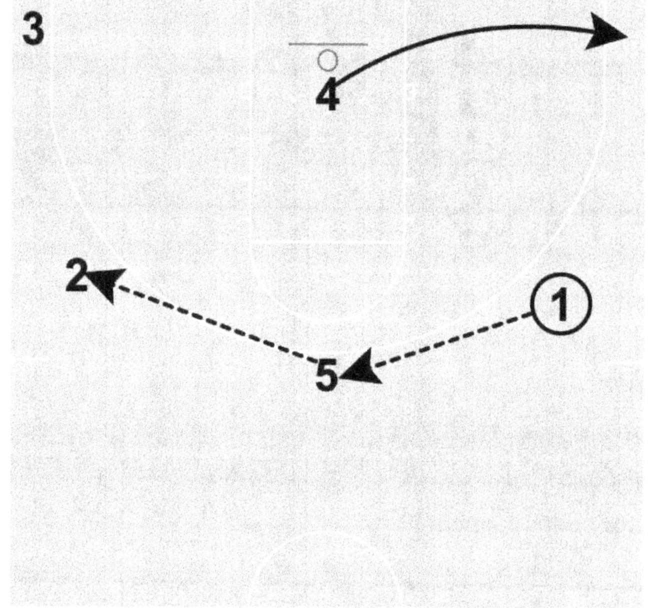

Diagram 1:

After 4 rim runs, he fills the open corner.

1-5-2 reverse of the ball.

5 Out Transition
Elbow Screen Away with DHO (Dribble Handoff)

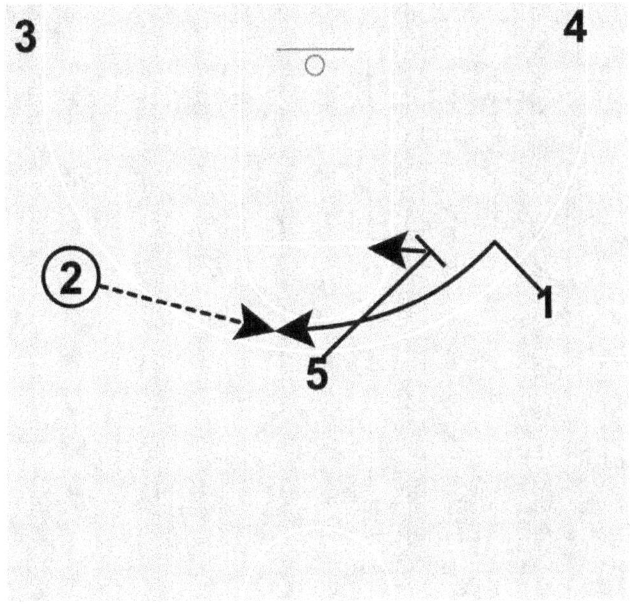

Diagram 2:

5/1 down screen.

5 spins back to weak elbow.

2-1 pass

5 Out Transition
Elbow Screen Away with DHO (Dribble Handoff)

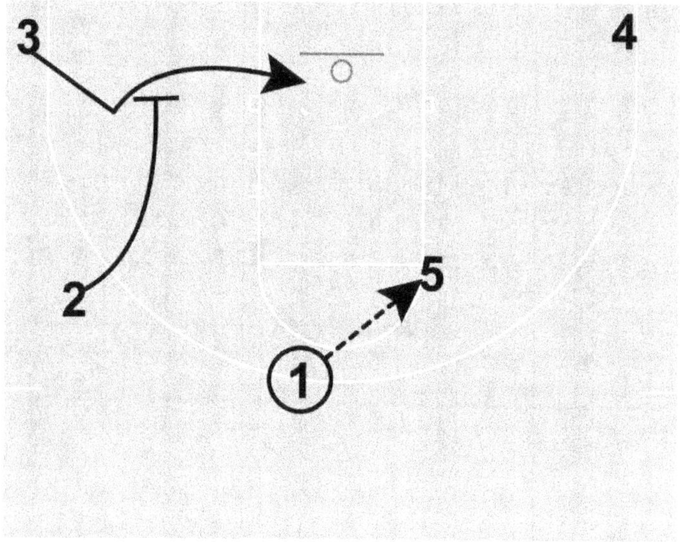

Diagram 3:

1-5 pass at pinch post.

2/3 down screen.

3 rejects 2's screen and cuts backdoor.

5 Out Transition
Elbow Screen Away with DHO (Dribble Handoff)

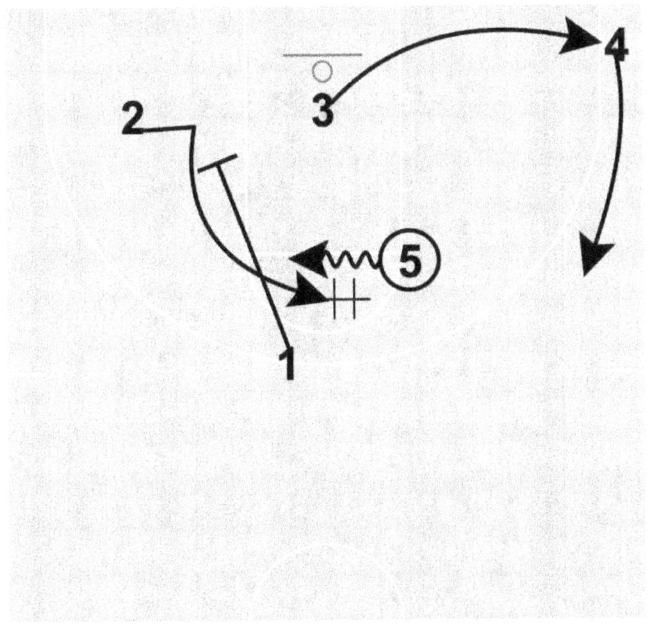

Diagram 4:

If 3 does not receive a pass, 4 lifts to the wing and 3 fills the corner.

1/2 down screen.

5/2 DHO (Dribble Handoff).

5 Out Transition
Elbow Screen Away with DHO (Dribble Handoff)

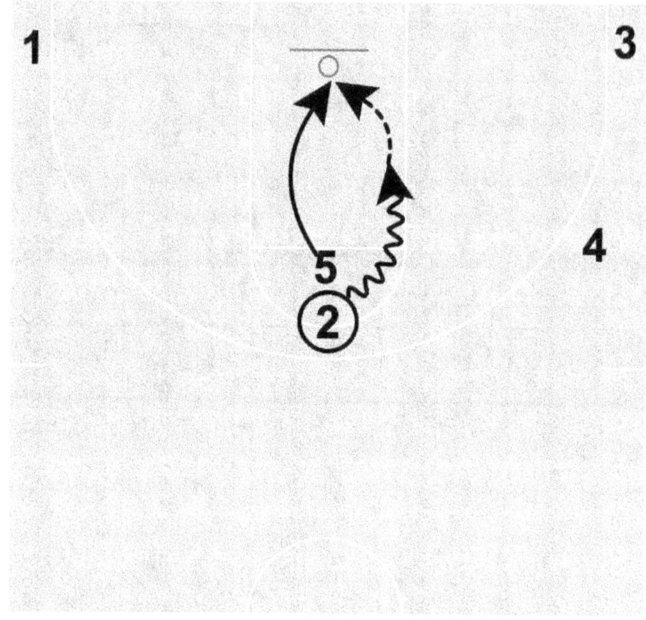

Diagram 5:

5 rolls to score.

2 makes a play.

2-5 pass for score if 5 open.

Chapter 6
5 Out Transition
Elbow Split with DHO

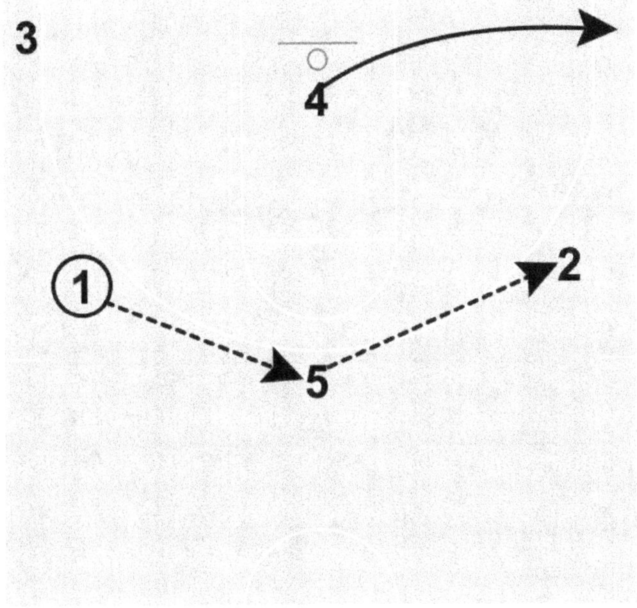

Diagram 1:

4 clears to open corner if he does not receive the ball in transition.

1-5-2 reverse of the ball.

5 Out Transition
Elbow Split with DHO

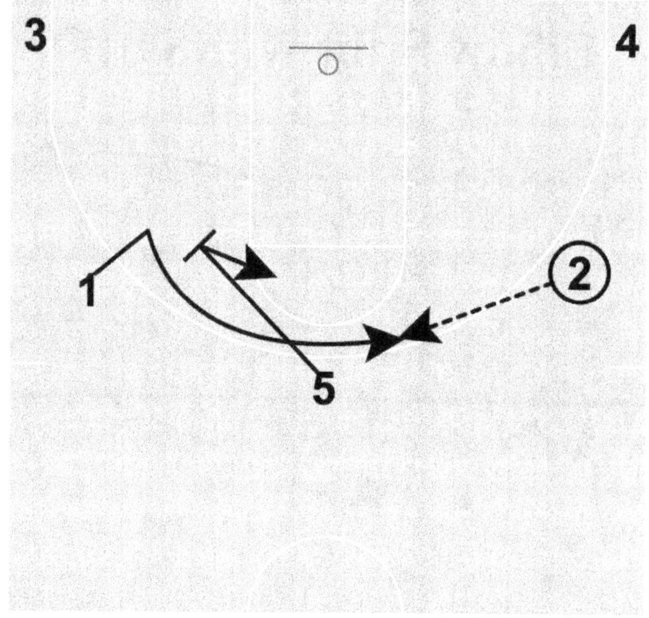

Diagram 2:

5/1 down screen.

2-1 pass.

5 spaces to the weak elbow.

5 Out Transition
Elbow Split with DHO

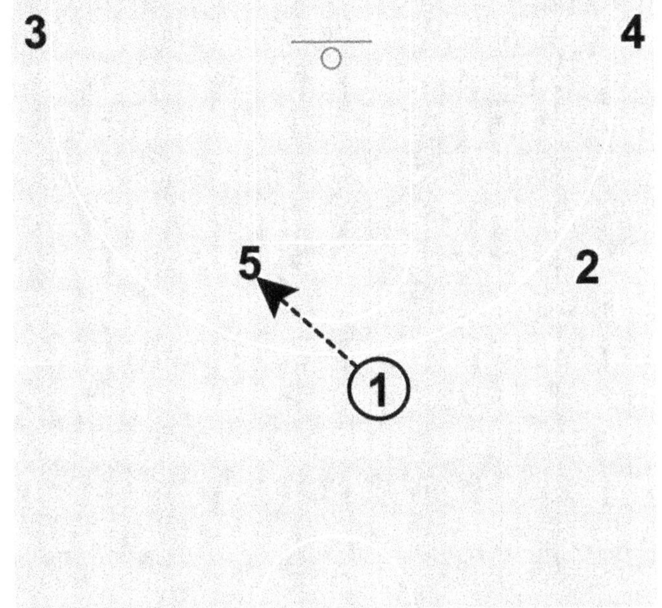

Diagram 3:

1-5 pass in pinch post.

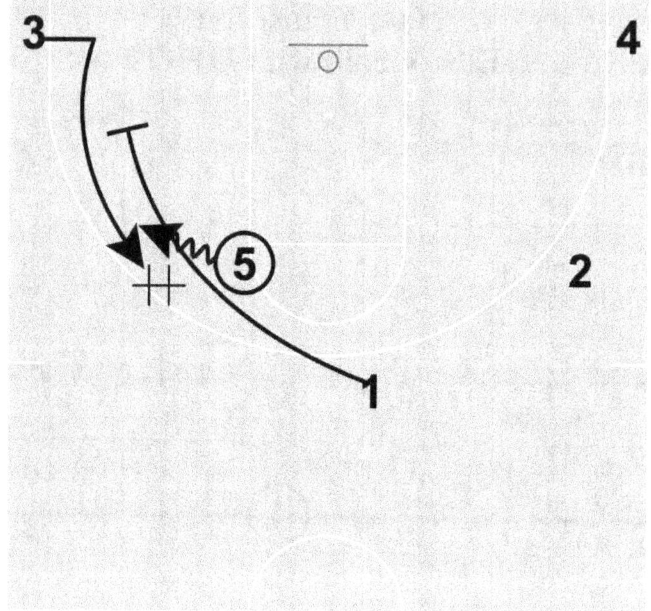

Diagram 4:

1/3 down screen.

5-3 DHO.

5 Out Transition
Elbow Split with DHO

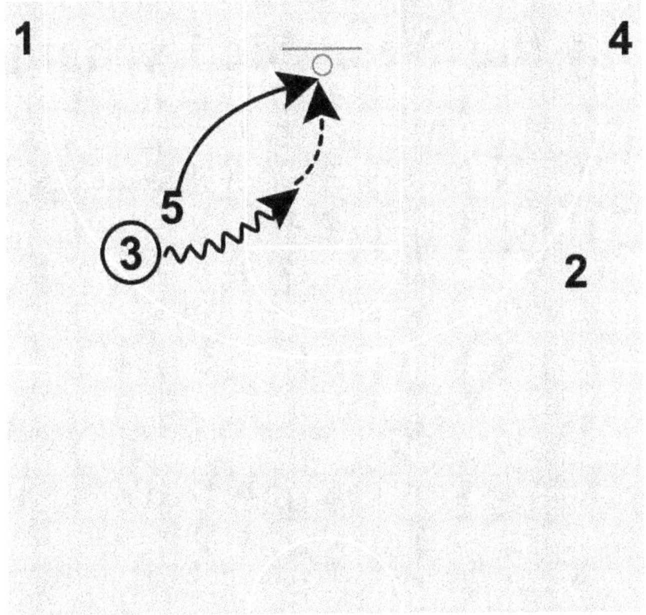

Diagram 5:

5 rolls to score.

3 drives to make a play.

3-5 pass for score if open.

Chapter 7
5 Out Transition
Play the Weakside Exchange

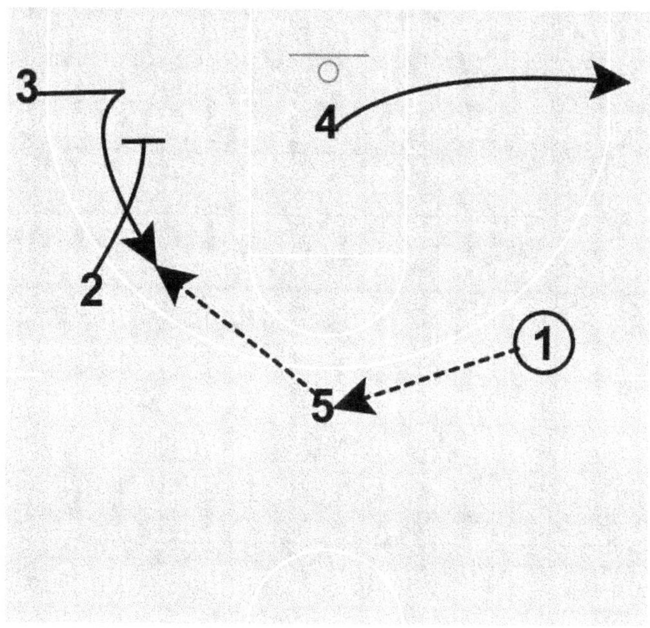

Diagram 1:

If 4 is not open, he fills the open corner.

1-5 pass.

2/3 down screen.

5-3 pass for J.

Note:

3 accepts 2's down screen.

5 Out Transition
Play the Weakside Exchange

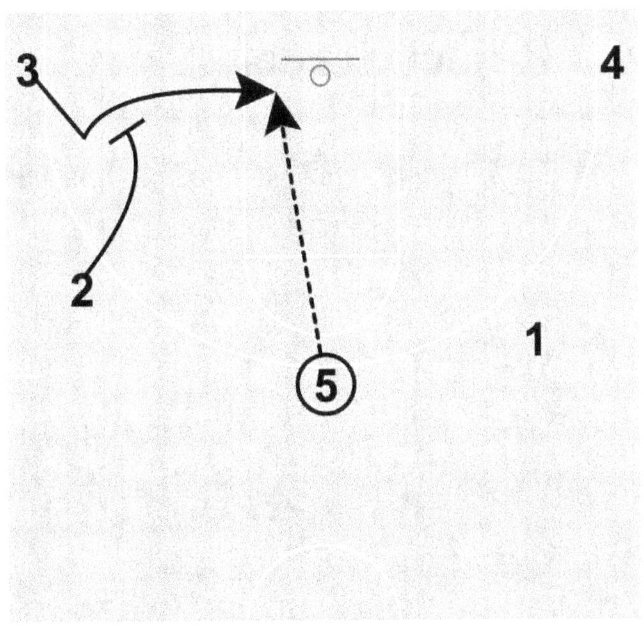

Diagram 2:

2/3 down screen.

3 rejects 2's down screen.

5-3 pass for a score on 3's back cut.

Note:

3 can curl over the top of 2.

2 can slip screen and back cut.

Chapter 8
5 Out Transition
Reject Screen Away

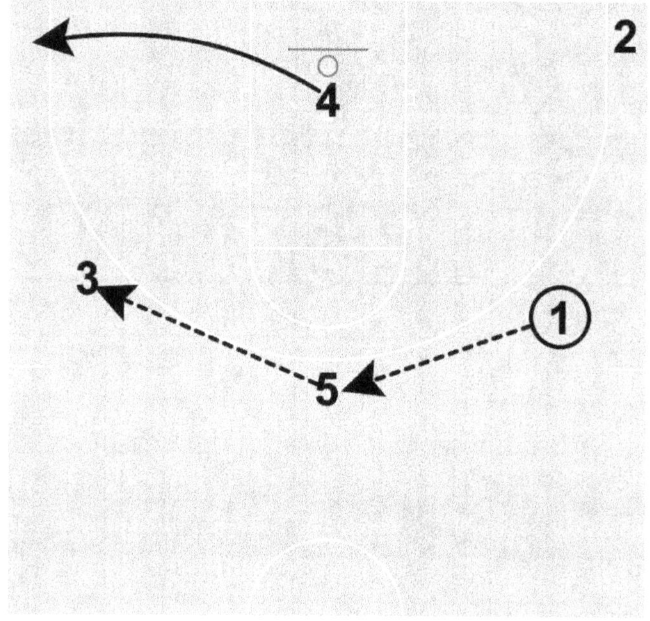

Diagram 1:

4 rim runs, pressures the rim and then fills the open corner if no pass.

1-5-3 reverse of the ball.

5 Out Transition
Reject Screen Away

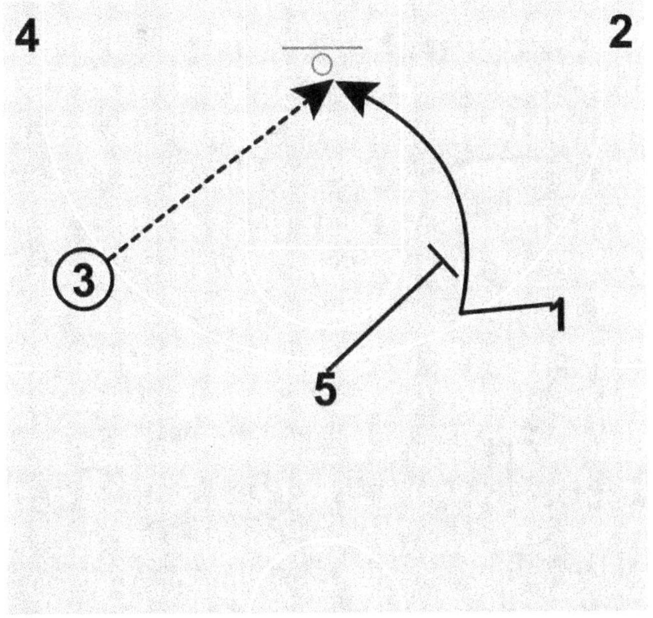

Diagram 2:

5/1 down screen.

1 rejects screen.

3-1 pass for a score on back cut.

Chapter 9
5 Out Transition
Screen Away and Roll

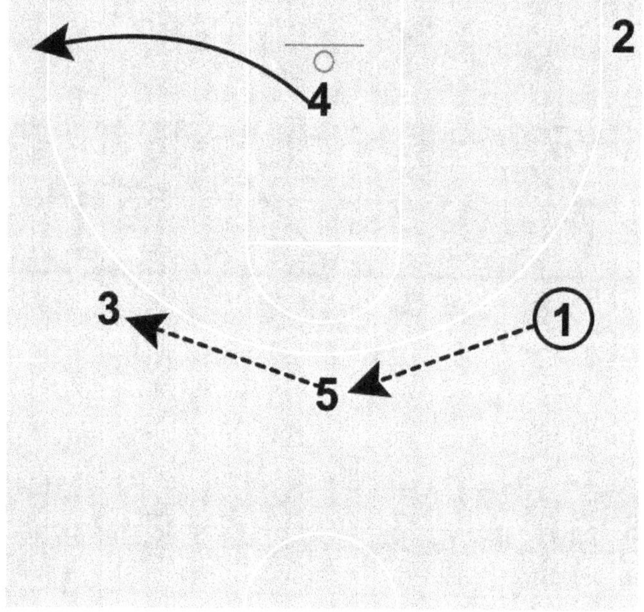

Diagram 1:

4 rim runs, pressures the rim and fills open corner if no pass.

1-5-3 reverse of the ball.

5 Out Transition
Screen Away and Roll

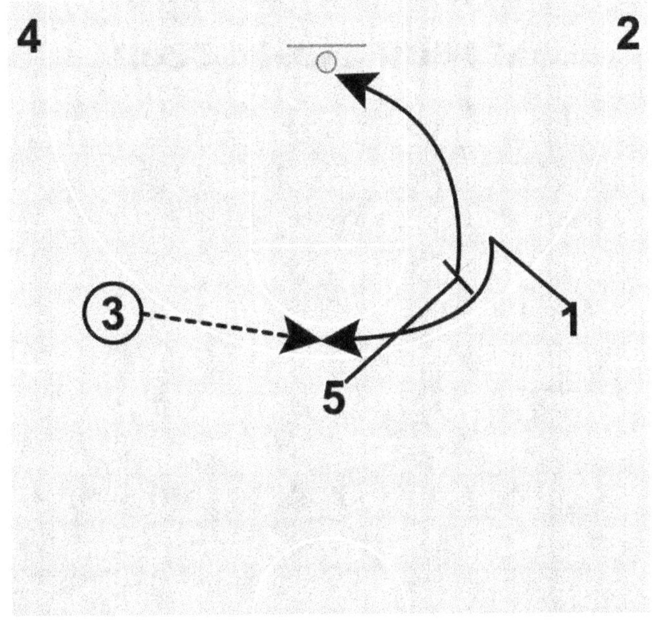

Diagram 2:

5/1 down screen.

3-1 pass for J.

5 rolls to score.

Note:

If 5 is open on the roll, 3-5 direct pass is an option also.

Chapter 10
5 Out Transition
Screen Re-Screen

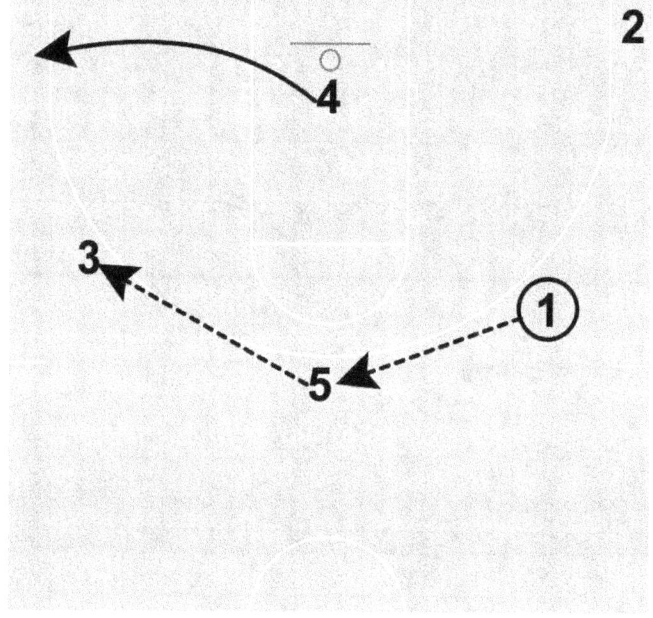

Diagram 1:

4 rim runs, pressure the rim, and then fills the open corner if no pass.

1-5-3 reverse of the ball.

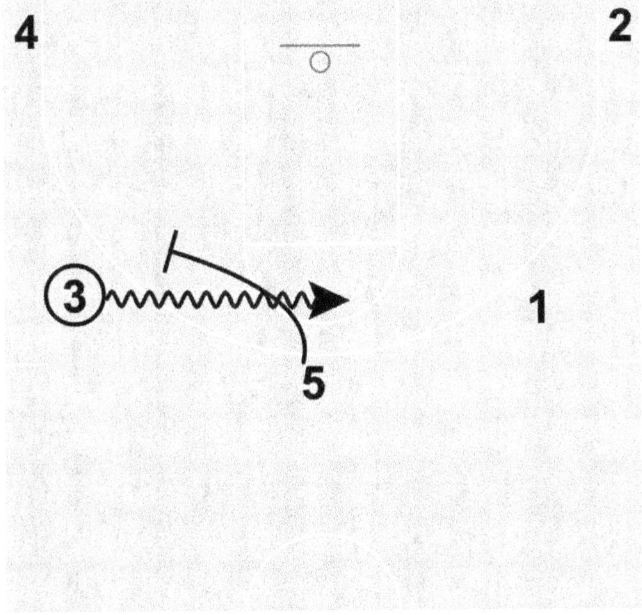

Diagram 2:

5/3 SOB (Screen on Ball).

3 drives the ball.

5 Out Transition
Screen Re-Screen

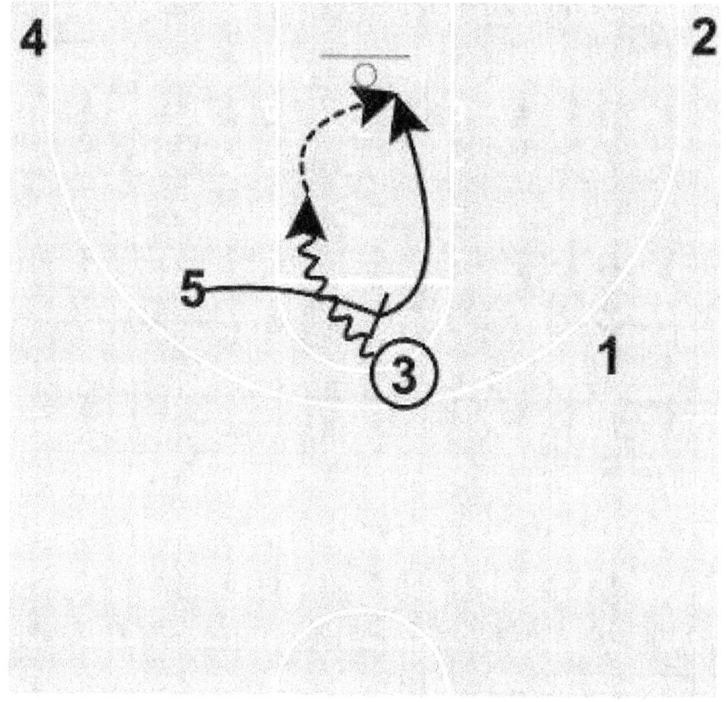

Diagram 3:

5/3 SOB.

3 drives to make a play.

5 rolls to score.

3-5 pass for score if open.

Chapter 11
5 Out Transition
Stagger to Horns Dribble at Backdoor

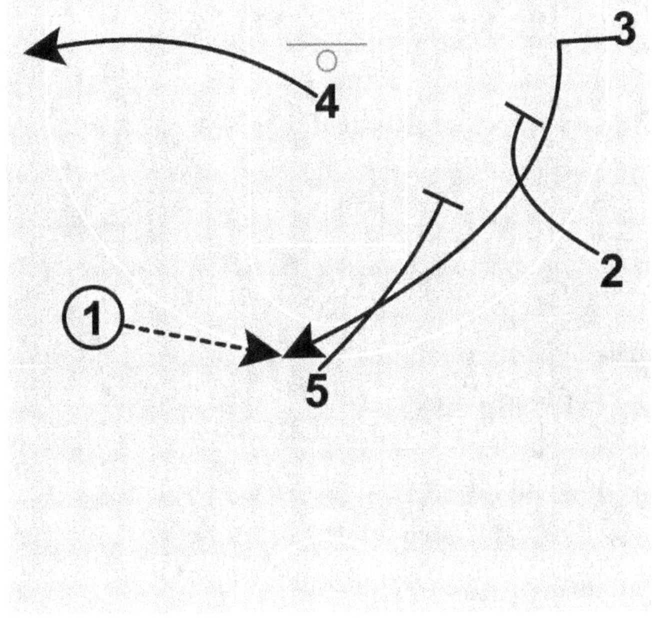

Diagram 1:

4 pressures the rim and fills the open corner if not open.

2+5/3 staggered down screen.

1-3 pass.

5 Out Transition
Stagger to Horns Dribble at Backdoor

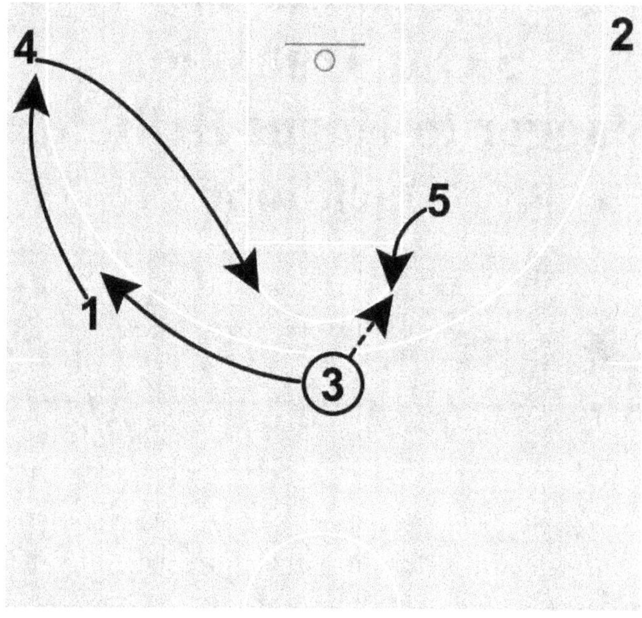

Diagram 2:

5 spaces to pinch post area.

4 fills opposite pinch post area.

1 fills the corner on his side.

2 fills the corner on his side.

3-5 pass at pinch post area.

5 Out Transition
Stagger to Horns Dribble at Backdoor

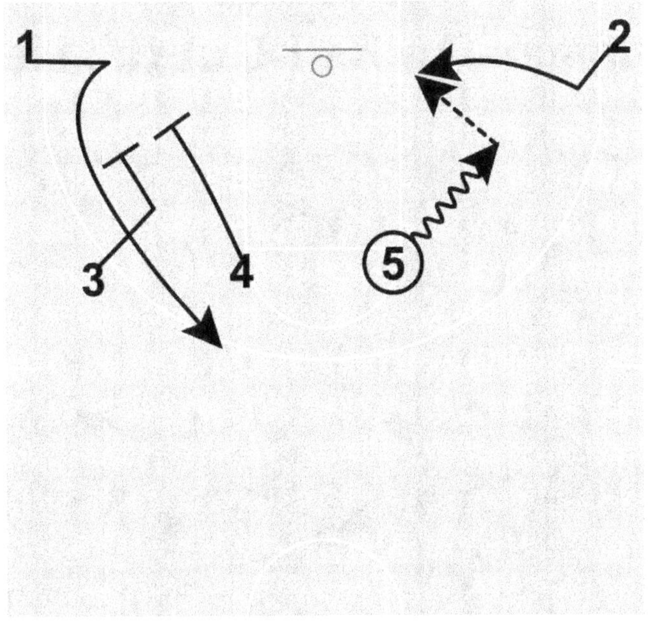

Diagram 3:

3+4/1 staggered/double down screen.

5 dribbles at 2.

2 cuts back door.

5-2 pass for score.

Chapter 12
5 Out Transition
Stagger-On Ball-Cut the Help

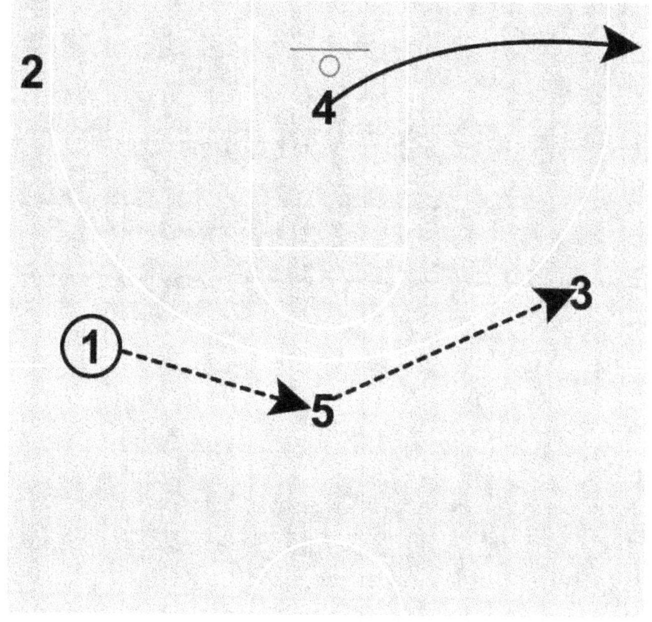

Diagram 1:

If 4 does not receive a pass, he clears to the open corner.

1-5-3 reverse of the ball.

5 Out Transition
Stagger-On Ball-Cut the Help

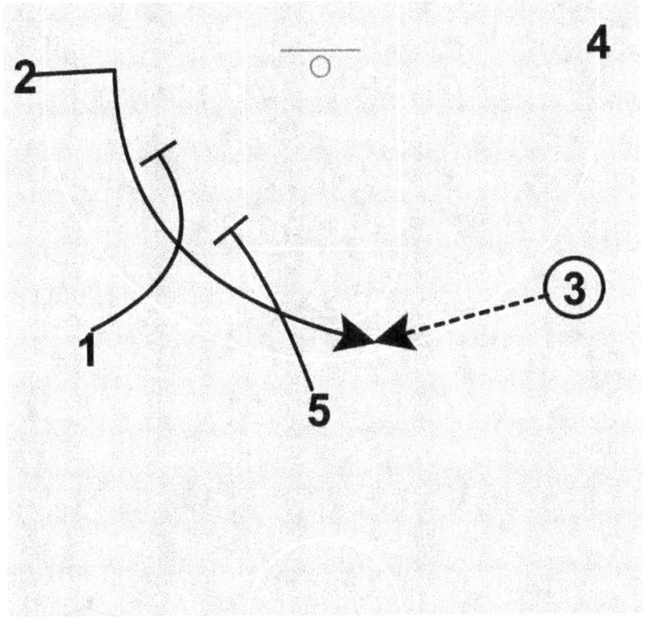

Diagram 2:

1+5/2 staggered down screen.

3-2 pass for J.

5 Out Transition
Stagger-On Ball-Cut the Help

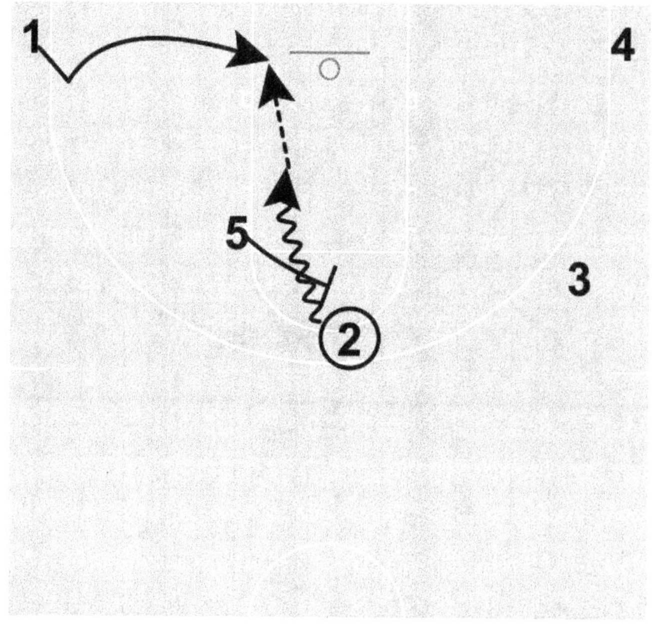

Diagram 3:

5/2 SOB.

2 drives to score.

1 cuts the help.

2-1 pass for score.

Chapter 13
5 Out Transition
Reverse of Ball Denied-Play the Other Way

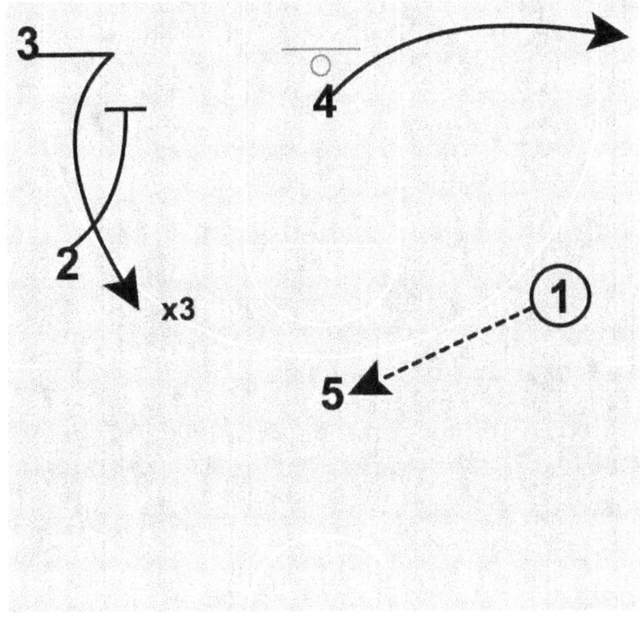

Diagram 1:

4 rim runs, pressures the rim and fills open corner if he does not receive the ball.

2/3 down screen.

1-5 pass.

5 Out Transition
Reverse of Ball Denied-Play the Other Way

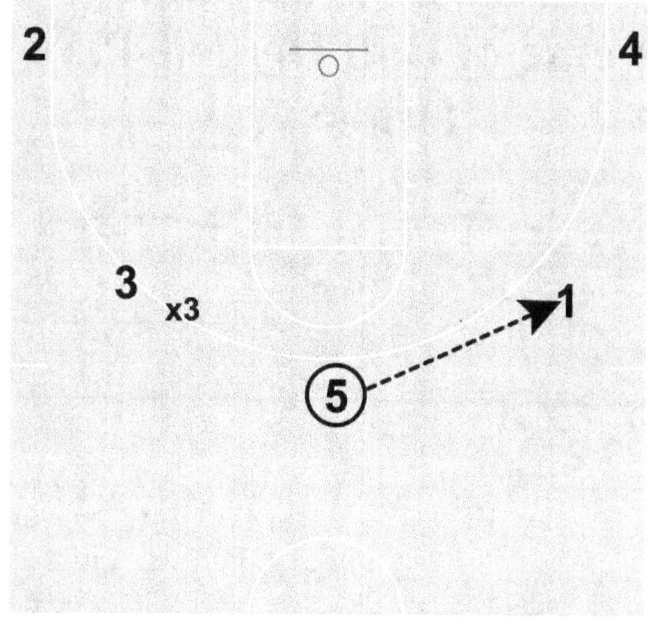

Diagram 2:

If 5 cannot reverse the ball to 3:

5-1 pass.

5 Out Transition
Reverse of Ball Denied-Play the Other Way

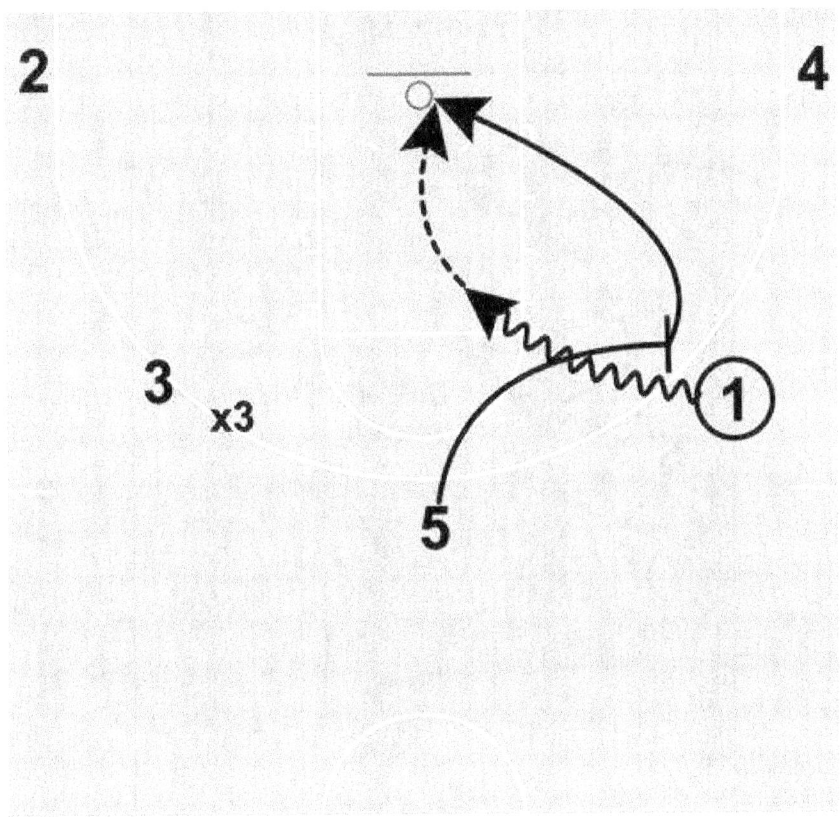

Diagram 3:

5-1 pass.

5/1 SOB (Screen on Ball)

5 rolls to score.

1 drives to make a play.

1-5 pass for score if open.

5 Out Transition
Miscellaneous Drags
Empty Drag

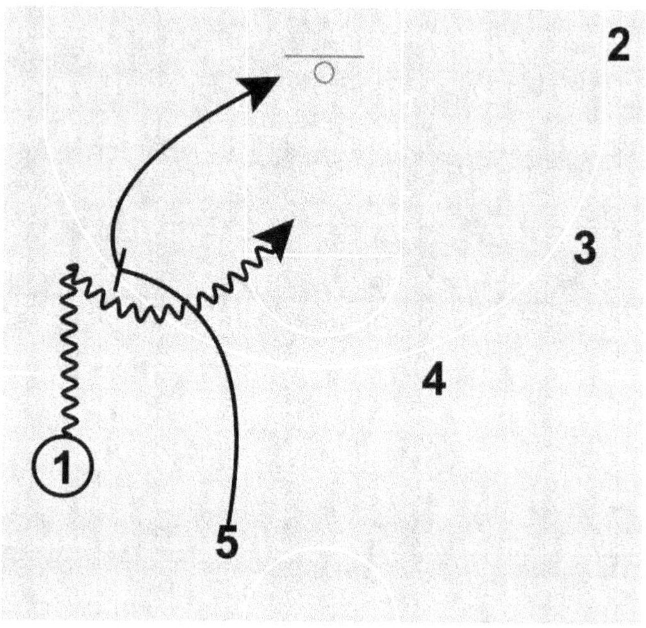

Diagram 1:

1 advances the ball in the outer third of the court.

5/1 SOB in transition.

1 drives to make a play.

5 rolls to score.

Note:

The strong side corner is empty and the floor is spaced.

5 Out Transition
Spread Drag

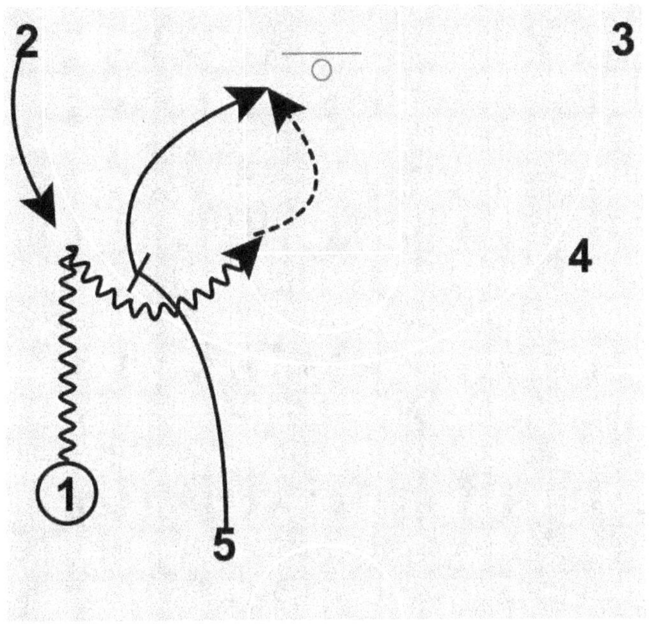

Diagram 1:

1 advances the ball in the outer third of the court.

5/1trail SOB.

1 drives to make a play.

5 rolls to score.

2 runs the arc or lifts from the corner.

5 Out Transition
Double Drag

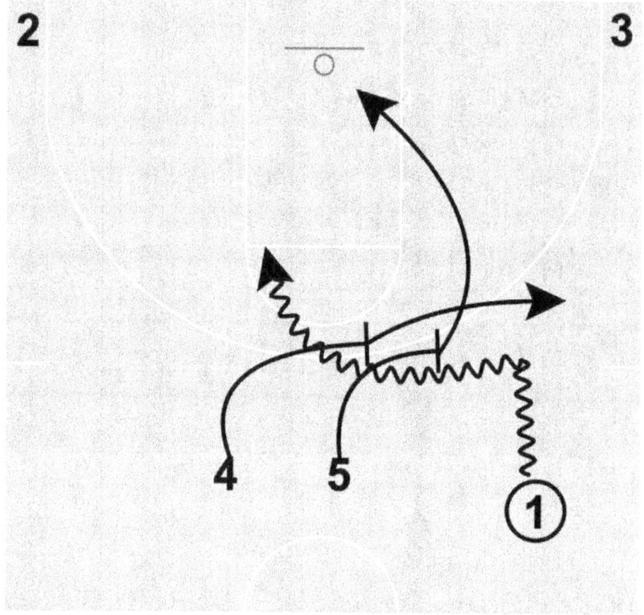

Diagram 1:

5+4/1 double drag screen in transition.

1 drives to make a play.

5 rolls to score.

4 spaces to open area.

Note:

The coach can designate between 2 and 3 who runs the arc and who cuts the help.

5 Out Transition
Double Drag

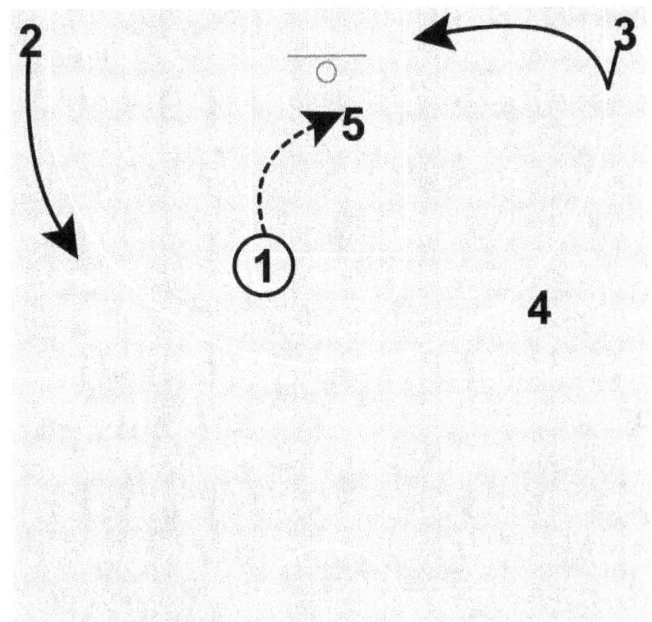

Diagram 2:

1-5 pass for score if open.

Note:

The coach can designate between 2 and 3 who runs the arc and who cuts the help.

5 Out Transition
Get Action

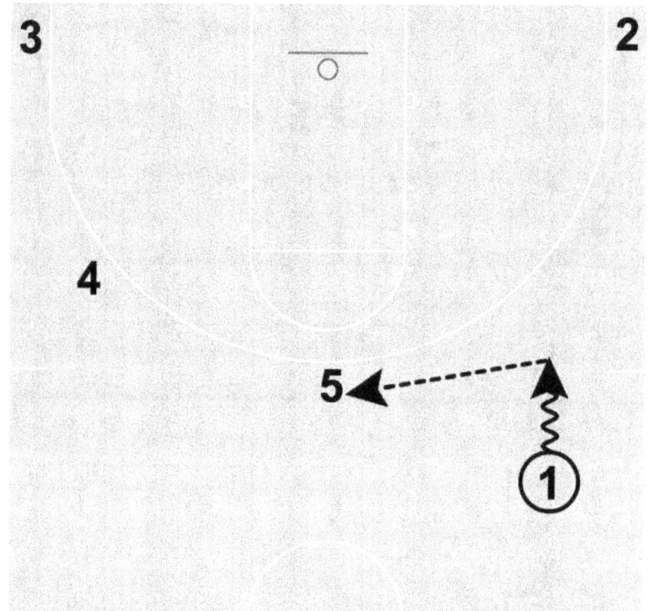

Diagram 1:

1-5 reverse of the ball

5 Out Transition
Get Action

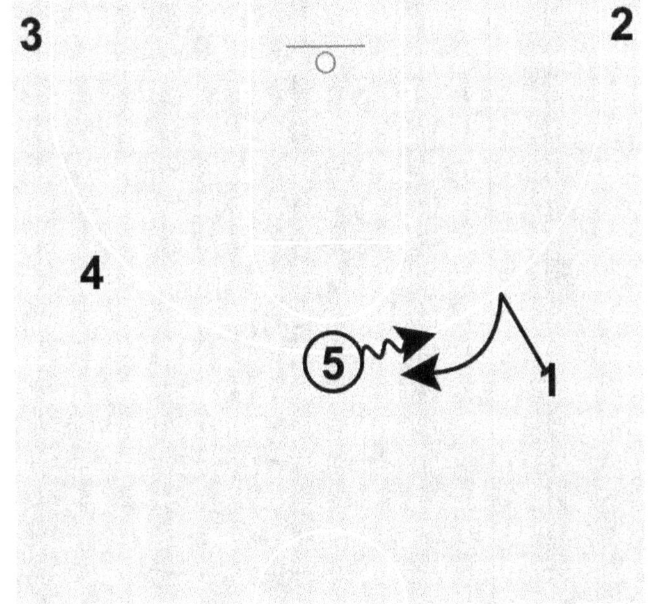

Diagram 2:

5-1 DHO.

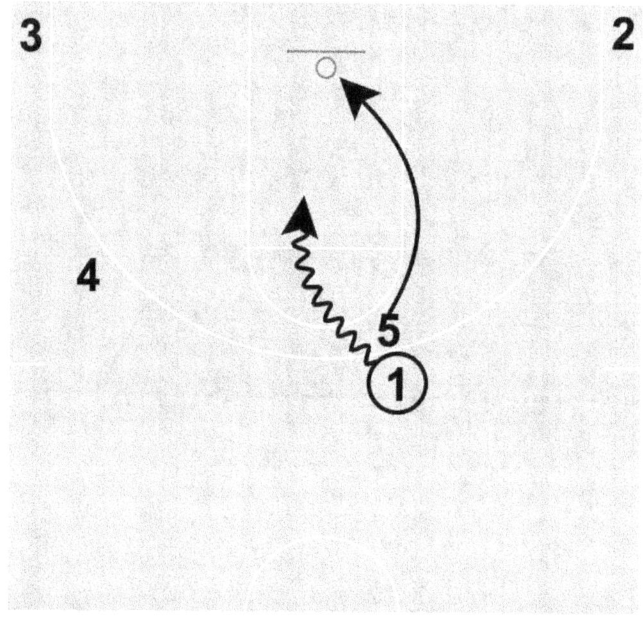

Diagram 3:

5 rolls to score.

1 drives to make a play.

Note:

The coach can designate who runs the arc and who cuts the help between 2, 3, and 4.

2 Man Game: Offensive phrase used to describe "shooter-opposite post."

3 Man Game: Offensive phrase used to describe weakside screening/cutting with three offensive players.

4-Second Sprint: The first way a post player can get open is by sprinting from his opponent's basket to his basket area in four seconds and then initiating his sealing action.

9 to 3's or U-ing: A drill used to practice the lunge step to control your defender's feet in the post. The post player starts at 6 0'clock. He steps to an imaginary offensive post at 12 o'clock. He then pins and spins, utilizing a lunge step into his sealing action. From 12 o'clock, the offensive post now takes two lunge steps to the right to 3 o'clock, four lunge steps to the left to 9 o'clock, and two final lunge steps to the right back to 12 o'clock.

- The knee must come above the hip on a lunge step. Also, the challenge is to maintain a proper posting stance with hands held high and out to call for the ball.

Alley Cut: (The Alley is the area below the blocks and behind the basket)

Another effective way for a post to get open is to cut under the basket opposite the dribbler. In other words, as the dribbler drives into the lane, the post moves opposite the ball but under the goal using the split line as a reference point.

Alley: Offensive term that refers to the area from just outside the backboard on the baseline.

Angle of Recovery: Defensive term that describes the direction the defender takes to improve position.

Arc Cut: Another way a post player can get open. When the ballhandler drives the ball from the middle of the floor to the baseline, and the post defender helps on the drive, the offensive post sprints to the three-point line on the wing to be a receiver.

Atomic Bomb: Offensive phrase that describes an uncontested transition layup of a steal or long rebound.

Attempts: Offensive term used to describe the number of times a team will get to play a live situation in practice situations.

Ball Call: Defensive term used when closing out to a player with the ball.

Ball Man, Front Man, Help Man: Defensive phrase used to describe the line of defenders to the basket; ball defender, post defender, basketball protector, or help man.

Ball Screen: When a teammate sets a screen on the dribbler, the screener's butt faces in the direction he would like the ball handler to dribble.

Barkley Dribble: Offensive term that refers to backing your defender down into the post area using a dribble drop and taking your defender in at least two directions: either up and then down or down and then up before making a post move.

Baseline Zone: Generic basketball phrase that describes the area below the free throw line extended divided by the split line.

Basket Retreat: Defensive phrase used to describe recovery in transition for the first player back. The player will retreat all the way to the lane area to be the protector.

Beat His Feet with Your Feet: See Lunge Step or Step Over.

Black: Defensive term or verbal command for trapping in the post.

Blind Pig: Offensive phrase that describes a high post entry from a weak side flash by a post player with quick back door cuts for scoring opportunities.

Blitz Down: Foul before:15 left on the shot clock.

Blitz Up: Foul immediately.

Blue: Verbal command that calls for soft pressure, usually in the backcourt in pressing situations.

Boxes: Describes the areas on the floor our defender is jamming and directing the ballhandler, both corners, both wings, and the top of the key.

Bring It: Offensive term post players use to tell the passer he has his defender sealed on the high side and to break the angle with a dribble toward the baseline to improve his passing angle; Also referred to as **"baseline bounce."**

Build Your Wall: Defensive term that describes a post defender in the post after an offensive player has caught the ball in the post or near the basket.

Building a Shelf: Extending an armbar to an opponent's chest to initiate a sealing action. (See Nelson to a Pollard)

Bulldog Action: After a mid-low post pass, a player will screen for the mid-low post receiver and play a two-man game in the mid-low post area.

Call Down: Offensive phrase that describes running the called set or quick hit at the end of the shot clock.

Call Up: Offensive phrase that describes running the called set or quick hit at the beginning of the shot clock.

Calls/Quick Hits: Offensive term that refers to offensive sets or plays.

Celtic Action: Offensive phrase that refers to movement after a mid-low post feed. Also referred to as X screen and slip. The player who fed the post screens at the elbow for the player in the middle third or top of the key area and then slips to the basket. The remaining players run the arc and cut the help. The coach can designate who cuts the help and who runs the arc.

Charge: Defensive/Offensive term that refers to a defender standing his ground, absorbing contact, and legally taking the hit from a driving offensive player.

Chest to the Corner: This is a technique a mid to low post offensive player incorporates when he is being fronted or defended on the high side.

Close Out: Defensive phrase that describes attacking a ballhandler with a live dribble, "hands up, weight back, feet moving!"

College Lane, AKA Lane or The Paint: Refers to the area on a basketball court underneath the basket bounded by the baseline and the foul line; Usually painted (although unpainted on some courts with painted perimeters), it is a critical area on the court, where much of the action takes place in a game. The college lane is 12' wide.

Contest Shot, Defend Drive: Defensive phrase that describes the physical approach to a closeout.

Corner Cut: Offensive term that refers to the movement of a player feeding the mid-low post and spacing or moving to the strong side corner.

Curl Cut: Offensive term that describes the cut an offensive player makes off a screen when the cutter is being chased in his footsteps by the defense.

D & D: Baseline drive and drift

Dead Call: Defensive term used by a defender guarding the basketball when his man kills or picks up his dribble.

Deflection: Generic basketball term that refers to a tip of the basketball by a defensive player on a pass.

Deny: Defensive term that describes preventing an opponent from catching a pass.

Diagonal Retreat: Defensive phrase that refers to perimeter player(s) in defensive transition or in the blue press. The player(s) will retreat to the mid-court area to meet their man as high up on the floor as possible, just inside the timeline of the backcourt.

Dig: A defensive term used to describe attacking the offensive player with an additional defensive player when he dribbles the ball.

Dive: Post back door.

Double Screen: Offensive term that refers to two screeners that come together to set a screen.

Drag: Offensive term used to describe a dribble entry.

Dribble Entry: Offensive term that describes a pressure release or wing entry other than via a pass to initiate the offense.

Dump Pass: Offensive term that refers to a pass to a teammate, usually on a drive to the basket, AKA "dime."

Early Offense: Offensive phrase used to describe transition game from the fast break to half-court offense.

Elbow Retreat: Defensive phrase used to describe defensive transition or in the soft press. The player(s) will retreat in transition to the defensive elbow to pick up his man.

Euro Screen: Offensive phrase that describes a type of screen with the screener's butt facing toward the basket.

Fade Cut: Offensive term that describes the cut an offensive player makes off a screen when the cutter's defender cheats under the screen; the cutter starts to curl and, at the level of the screen and when he sees the defender cheat under, pushes back away from the cut. Also known as a "flair cut" or "flair."

Fake Trap: Defensive phrase used to describe our help side rotation. A defensive player will lose vision on his man and run at the dribbler until the offensive player picks up the ball or retreats away from the basket. Once the offensive player has killed his dribble, the defensive player will rotate back to his man.

Foot Angles: Defensive term that describes which foot is up in a staggered stance; left foot on the left side of the floor and right foot on the right side of the floor.

Full Deny or Faceguard: Verbal command that calls for a defensive position that is directly between your opponent and the ball, usually in pressing situations where the defense needs a quick turnover.

Gap(s): Generic basketball term that refers to the area between defenders.

Go Away, Come Back: Another simple yet effective way to get open in the post is to start away as if anticipating the reverse of the ball and V-Back to the ball. The key here is to beat your opponent to the punch, hold your seal, and only come back as far as you need to receive the ball.

Grenade Action: An offensive phrase describing player movement after a mid-low post feed. The player who received the pass from the perimeter in the mid-low post area will dribble handoff (DHO) to a player on the perimeter, usually on the strong wing or top of the key area. This is common in the NBA. Big-on-little or post-on-perimeter dribble handoffs (DHO) out of the post area in tight quarters are hard to guard.

Halfway to Pivot: Defensive term that describes defensive post position with a hand and foot in front of the offensive post preventing a direct pass into the offensive post.

Hammer Action: On Baseline Drive, a weakside offensive player screens for the perimeter player spacing to drift corner or weak corner.

Hands Up, Weight Back, Feet Moving: Defensive phrase that describes proper techniques for a closeout.

Help Call: Defensive term shouted to let his teammates know that he has been beaten off the dribble point of attack (POA).

Help Position: Defensive Phrase that refers to the act of getting away from the man you are guarding and assisting the player guarding the basketball.

Help Side or Weakside: Defensive term that refers to the side of the court opposite the basketball.

Help the Helper: Defensive term that describes a defender's responsibility when a teammate slides to be a primary helper on a drive or post feed.

High Hand: Offensive term post players use to tell the passer he has a defensive post sealed on the low side and to pass the ball to the hand away from the baseline and defense.

High Hands: Defensive term that describes the position we want hands at the end of a closeout to the ballhandler.

I-Cut: Another way a post player can get open. When the ballhandler drives the ball from the wing towards the baseline, the offensive post runs the lane line to the elbow to be a receiver. If the dribbler crosses the split line, the post should be moving to the opposite side of the goal. He then begins his sealing action on anyone near him.

In the Hole: Offensive term that refers to a player lining up under the basket.

Isolation: Offensive term used to describe an opportunity for an offensive player to go one on one with his defender.

Jam Down/Pin Down: Offensive Phrase that describes the act of setting a down screen for a teammate to get him open to safely receive the basketball.

Jam the Ball: Defensive phrase used to describe closely guarded or imposing your will on the dribbler.

Jam Up: Offensive term that describes screening from the basket out.

Jump Switch Your Feet: An offensive post phrase that describes the footwork when the pass is made from the wing to the top of the key on a second pass direct opportunity. The post player goes from "numbers to the ball" to switching his feet so his chest faces the opposite sideline while holding his seal on his defender.

Kill the Play: Defensive phrase that refers to doing what is necessary to stop an opponent's scoring opportunity.

Kill the Thigh: See Lunge Step or Step Over

Laker Cut: Offensive term that refers to the movement of players after a mid-low post feed; passer cuts through the lane above post, weak post or 4-man cuts the help to the weak block, and perimeter players rotate into the vision of the post player who received the initial pass.

Laker: When shooter-opposite-post in the 2-man game and the passer feeds the post, the passer cuts through above the second hash mark on the lane line, cut the help to the weak mid-post area with a post or perimeter, and the remaining players run the arc.

Line of the Ball: Generic basketball phrase that describes an imaginary line between the passer and offensive receiver.

Load: Fill or space to a specific area.

Lunge Step or Step Over: AKA "Beat His Feet with Your Feet": The offensive post player seals with his feet by taking the foot closest to the defender and stepping over the defender's foot. This gives the post player control of the defender's feet, and a sealing stance can be assumed. The rule is the offensive post player's knee must get above his knee and then over his opponent's leg.

Middle Motion: Offensive phrase that describes cross-screen/down-screen; Weak action in Open Hand and Basic.

Mini-Lane/Dunk Box: Describes the area in the lane below the logo and between the lane lines and baseline.

Moon: A defensive term that refers to a post defender breaking contact with his offensive player and moving either high to low or low to high, depending on where the ball is in the mid-to-low post area.

Nail: Generic basketball term that refers to the middle of the free-throw line.

Naked Flash: Another way for a post player to get open in the post. Oftentimes, a post player can get open by simply flashing to the ball from the weak side. It is pure deception. Ben Jacobson's post players at Northern Iowa do an especially good job of this maneuver.

NBA Lane: The key, officially referred to as the free throw lane by the National Basketball Association (NBA) bounded by the end line or baseline, free-body lines, and the foul line; Usually painted (although unpainted on some courts with painted perimeters), it is a critical area on the court, where much of the action takes place in a game.

Nelson to a Pollard: Extending an armbar to an opponent's chest to initiate a sealing action. (See Building a Shelf)

- With the change in the rules and how the game is officiated, post players may have to adjust using the armbar in their sealing action.
- In college, to adjust to the change in the rules, a post player can use his hips and legs to initiate contact and begin the sealing action.

Off the Line of the Ball: Defensive phrase that describes the ball-you-man principle or basic defensive position from the passer to the receiver. The defensive position is between the passer and receiver, but one step off the line or toward the basket.

Oscar Call: Offensive term used to signal for a blind pass to the offensive goal when a player has a run-out.

Paint Call: Offensive term that refers to aggressively driving the basketball to the lane area to score, be fouled, or both.

Passing Angle: Offensive term that describes the best or safest path for the ball to be thrown.

Perimeter Zone: Generic basketball phrase that describes the area above the free throw line extended.

Pick and Pop: This is an offensive phrase that describes one offensive player screening for the ballhandler and after his screen spacing to an open area of the floor.

Pick and Roll: Setting a ball screen and rolling to score is different from just rolling. There must be intent and aggressiveness to get to the basket, put your body on someone to seal, then catch and finish simply.

Pig: Offensive term that refers to a high post entry with quick back door cuts for scoring opportunities.

Pistol Action: Dribble handoff (DHO) to a ball screen.

Piston Action: Offensive phrase that refers to the movement of players after a mid-low post feed. After the mid-low post pass, the passer and player at the top of the key meet at the elbow. The player at the top screens for the passer, and the passer cuts over the top of the screener to the basket. The screener spaces into the low post's vision. The remaining players run the arc and cut the help. The coach can designate who cuts the help and who runs the arc.

Play Ball, See Man: Defensive phrase that describes the mentality that a defender must use when playing help defense.

Pollard: This is a term we used referring to a posting stance wherein a player sitting in must be big three ways; wide feet, knees bent, back straight, head up, hands out and up like you are holding up; a pane of glass.

Post Entry: Offensive term that describes a pass to a post typically used as a pressure release to help initiate an offensive motion or set.

Post Entry: Pass to pinch post.

Power Step: Offensive phrase used to describe the movement or stride used to get beyond a defender.

Quick Flash: Offensive phrase that describes a cut by an offensive player who deviates from motion or a call to take advantage of a scoring opportunity by opening up to the basketball and moving into an open gap.

Quick Hits: Offensive term that refers to offensive sets or plays.

Raptor Action: An offensive phrase that refers to the movement of players after a mid-low post feed. After the mid-low post feed, the passer and player at the top of the key screen are away for the next player. The player being screened for now cuts the arc to get in the vision of the post receiver. As in Piston, Laker, and Celtic Action, the remaining players run the arc or cut the help. The coach may designate runners and cutters.

Rebounds Given Up: Defensive phrase used to describe an offensive rebound.

Recover to Position: Defensive phrase that describes where players must adjust relative to the ball and their man.

Red: Defensive term or verbal command for trapping on the perimeter.

Rotation: Movement by defender(s) to assist in stopping the basketball from penetrating to the goal or to cover up an open offensive player.

Rub: Offensive term used to describe an offensive player's cut off a teammate to get open.

Run Him Off the Arc: Defensive term that describes a long closeout, usually to an extremely good shooter influencing him to dribble instead of shoot the 3.

Run Out: Generic basketball phrase that describes a defender getting a jump on the offense by sprinting toward his own goal anticipating his team will secure the basketball.

Scramble: Defensive term used to describe an emergency situation when all defenders make an effort to stop the basketball, recover to position and rebuild the defense accepting the fact that each player may be in a miss match.

Screen: Offensive term used to describe the offensive player's movement to put his body on a teammate's defender to get him open to safely receive the basketball.

Seal Up for the Lob: If X5 fronts or plays on the high side of 5, 5 goes from "showing his numbers" to the ball to jump-switching his feet to hold his seal. 5's chest should now point to the corner, hold his seal, and release his seal as the ball passes over his head and away from the defense.

Seam: Generic basketball term that refers to the guard spots or lane line extended above the key.

Second Pass Direct: When 5 is being fronted or being guarded on the high side in the post, he can direct the ball to the top of the key by simply pointing to the top.

Sense of Urgency: Generic basketball term that describes showing a high level of awareness, resolve, and concentration to persevere during practice, game prep, or competition.

Sets: Offensive term that refers to Quick Hits or Calls.

Shake Up: Offensive phrase used to describe a perimeter player's cut or movement in an overload situation from corner to wing in standard side ball screen motion or side pick and roll.

Shell Defense: Generic defensive basketball phrase that describes all defensive teaching situations, i.e., screens, patterns, technique, used to build team defense.

Shooter-Opposite-Post: Offensive phrase used to describe establishing the two-man game on the ball side of the court. The shooter on the perimeter is spaced away from the post that is set up in the mid to low post.

Short Corner Step Out: Another way a post player can get open. When the ballhandler drives the ball from the wing toward the middle of the floor, the offensive post steps to the short corner, also referred to as the dunk spot, to be a receiver.

Short Corner: Offensive Phrase that refers to the area between the alley and deep corner; also where post players space on drives to the middle of the floor.

Shot Call: Defensive term used by an on-ball defender to alert teammates shot has been taken, and block outs are required.

Show Your Hands: Defensive term refers to keeping your hands high or elevated on a drive after a closeout so the officials can see them.

Shut Down the Ball/Shut 'em Down: Defensive phrase used to describe taking away middle penetration via the dribble or the pass. We want to force the basketball to the outside and the baseline.

Site Check: Defensive phrase that describes physically turning to look to determine if your man is going to the offensive glass.

Slip: Offensive term that describes an offensive player who fakes a screen or leaves from his screen early as his man helps to space to an open area to be an option or receiver to a pass.

Slow Trap: Defensive phrase used to describe a containment-type trap in the backcourt to slow the ball down. This trap will typically occur between the 1 man and one of the two post players in a press situation or against a hard-pushing point guard.

Split Line: Defensive phrase that refers to the imaginary line that divides the court down the center from goal to goal.

Stagger Screen: Offensive term that refers to 2 screeners that tandem with each other to set a screen off the ball.

Stay Action: Another way for a post player to get open. A post player who is on the weak block can effectively get open by anticipating the pass to the top of the key. The post player waits for the pass of the ball to the top of the key before he begins his sealing action. Making your defender think you are out of the play or action can go a long way to helping you get open on the ball side.

Step Up Screen: Offensive term that refers to a screen that occurs on the ballhandler with the screener's butt pointing to the baseline.

Straight Cut: Offensive term that describes offensive players cut when their defender gets caught up in the screen.

Stunt: Defensive term that describes faking or bluffing at the dribbler.

Swing the Ball: Offensive term that describes ball reversal or reversing the ball from one side of the court to the other.

Swing the Wings: Offensive phrase that describes crossing the wings under the basket or restricted area to the opposite wing area.

Swing: On dribble entry, wings swing or cross under the basket.

Switch/Fake Switch: Defensive terms used to describe how we want to cover screening situations, whether we help and recover or switch.

-Talk: Let teammate know that the screen is occurring, "switch or get through."

-Touch: The two defenders come together, leaving no space for slip.

-Take: Defend the offensive player you are switching onto.

Ten Pack: Warm up drill executing 5 layups from both sides of the floor; straight line, up and under, pull up, slide shot, euro step. We will also use all three types of balls.

Texas Two Step: Offensive phrase that defines footwork once the sealing action has been completed. After the post player has initiated contact and has sealed his defender, he now drives the defender back two quick steps to maintain contact and improve his scoring opportunity.

Trace the Ball/Bother the Ball: Defensive phrases that refer to active hands on the ball to create deflections and/or discourage a pass.

Up the Line of the Ball: Defensive phrase that describes the ball-you-man principle or basic defensive position from the passer to the receiver. The defensive position is between the passer and receiver, but toward the passer.

V-Back: Generic basketball phrase that describes a defensive player's angle of recovery back to help position.

V-Cut: An offensive term that refers to the cutter taking his defender one or two steps in one direction and then cutting in the opposite direction.

War: Generic basketball term that refers to the mentality players must take when there is a need to raise the intensity to the highest level.

Weave: An offensive term involving at least three players that describes a dribble handoff from players A to B and then B to C.

Wedge Screen: Screen for the screener.

Wheel: Wing backdoor to 2nd backdoor to post.

Whip Action: On baseline drive, big screens in for perimeter at the top of the key.

Wide Pin: Offensive term that refers to a down screen for a player in a baseline corner.

Wing Entry: Offensive term that describes a pass to the player on the wing to initiate an offensive motion or set.

Wolf Call: Generic basketball term used to alert dribbler a defender is coming from behind.

X Screen: Offensive term that refers to the movement of players after a low post feed; weak post or four-man dives to the weak block, passer screens for perimeter player at the top of the key and then slips to the basket.

Signs to Consider When Communicating with Players During a Game: Flex

Fade

Strong

Weak

Pipe/Zipper

Check

Go

(Out Front)
"X"

(Out Front)
Reverse

(Out Front)
Double Reverse

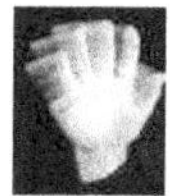 

(Out Front)

(Out Front)
Plow

(Over Head)
Opposite

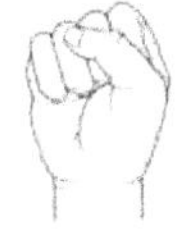 

↔

Call Up

(Play is run immediately)

Call Down

(Play is run at the end of the shot clock.)

About The Author

Marty Gross

Marty Gross, after 46 years of coaching college basketball, enters the next chapter in his basketball journey.

Gross spent the 2022-2023 season coaching at Missouri State University, helping the Bears to a 17-15 overall record.

Before the Bears, Gross spent 10 years at Texas A&M Corpus Christi in addition to a short 5-month stint at the University of St. Thomas on the women's side. Texas A&M Corpus Christi enjoyed one of its most successful seasons ever in 2015-16, rolling up 25 wins and advancing to the Southland Conference Championship game for the first time, and making three straight postseason appearances.

Gross spent 10 years at TAMUCC, four years at Wichita State, seventeen years at Rice University, nine years at Jacksonville University (Fla.), and four years at Birmingham Southern College (Ala.).

At Wichita State, Gross was instrumental in helping the Shockers win the 2011 NIT Championship with wins over a Klay Thompson-led Washington State team in the semi-finals and Alabama in the finals.

Gross began his collegiate coaching career at Birmingham-Southern College upon graduating from Jacksonville in 1977. During his four years in Birmingham, the Panthers were 103-27, captured three-consecutive Southern States Conference championships, competed in two national tournaments, and achieved a national ranking as high as second in the NAIA polls.

In addition to Birmingham Southern College, Gross also coached at his alma mater, Jacksonville University (FL). His first stint at Jacksonville was from 1981 to 1983. Gross then returned to Jacksonville in 1985 and spent the next seven years at the campus, including three seasons as the school's associate head coach.

Gross has been instrumental in helping cultivate the careers of 60 pros, including 14 from Texas A&M Corpus Christi, 13 from Wichita State University, 21 from Rice, eight from Jacksonville, and two from Birmingham Southern College.

While at Jacksonville, Gross teamed with former JU/Rutgers/New Jersey Nets coach and current television analyst Bob Wenzel, helping nurture the careers of six Dolphins selected in the NBA draft. Some of the more notable players include 1986 second-round pick (Denver) and former Orlando Magic general manager and current NBA consultant Otis Smith, 1987 first-round pick Ronnie Murphy (Portland), 1990 first-round selection and NBA Slam Dunk Champion Dee Brown (Boston) and 1992 second-round pick Tim Burroughs (Minnesota). In 1985-86, the Dolphins were 21-10, won the Sun Belt Conference Championship, and made an appearance in the NCAA tournament. In 1986-87, the Dolphins were 19-11 and received an NIT postseason bid.

At Rice, Gross coordinated recruiting and was involved extensively in all areas of the day-to-day operations of the men's basketball program, including fund-raising, player development, community outreach, scouting, and a daily practice focus on team defense. He also helped develop 21 Owls to the professional ranks, including NBA players Morris Almond (2007 First Round Utah Jazz), Mike Harris (Houston Rockets, Utah Jazz), Mike Wilkes (Orlando, Memphis, Milwaukee, Houston, San Antonio, Seattle), and Brent Scott (Indiana Pacers).

A native of Yankton, South Dakota, Gross was an all-state basketball player as a senior at Yankton Senior High School in 1973. He is a member of the Yankton Senior High School Hall of Fame and the National Association of Basketball Coaches. Gross also attends St. Mark's Episcopal Church and has been active in Athletes in Action and Fellowship of Christian Athletes and the Texas Association of Basketball Coaches.

Gross is married to Mary Pat Nelson, a native of Beaumont, Texas. The couple resides in Houston, Texas. In addition to "Transition Attack: 5 Out Transition", Gross' first book project was "A Systematic Approach to Teaching Post Play" also on Amazon and coachmartygross.org.

Gross Coached Players in the NBA/Professional Players

Islanders in the Pros
Chris Mast 6-6, 2012
Terence Jones 6-3, 2013
Zane Knowles 6-10, 2014
John Jordan 5-10, 2015
Bryce Douvier 6-7, 2016
Hameed Ali 6-3, 2016
Viktor Juricek 7-0, 2016
Rashawn Thomas 6-8, 2017
Joe Kilgore 6-5, 2018
Ehab Amin 6-4, 2018
Kareem South 6-2, 2019
Jake Babic 6-5, 2019
Elijah Schmidt 6-8, 2020
Tony Lewis 6-10, 2020

Shockers in the Pros
Gal Mekel 6-3, 2008 (Dallas Mavericks)
Phillip Thomasson 6-6 Forward, 2008
PJ Cousinard 6-4 Guard, 2008
Ramon Clemente   6-6, 2009
Mantas Griskenas 6-7, 2009
Clevin Hannah 5-11, 2010
Aaron Ellis 6-9, 2011
JT Durley 6-8, 2011
Gabe Blair 6-8, 2011
Garrett Stutz 7-0, 2012
Joe Ragland 6-0, 2012
David Kyles 6-3, 2012
Toure' Murry 6-5, 2012 (New York Knicks)

Owls in the Pros
Brent Scott, Center, 1992 (Indiana Pacers)
Marvin Moore, Guard, 1993
David Holmes, Guard, 1993
Adam Peakes, Guard, 1995

Tommy McGhee, Guard, 1996

J.J. Polk, Guard, 1997

Shaun Igo, Center, 1997

Jarvis Kelly Sanni, Forward, 1998

Robert Johnson, Guard, 1999

Jason Skaer, Forward, 1999

Alex Bougaieff, Center, 2000

Erik Cooper, Forward, 2001

Mike Wilks, Guard, 2001 (Orlando, Memphis, Milwaukee, Houston, San Antonio, Seattle)

T.J. McKenzie, Center, 2002

Yamar Diene, Center, 2004

Jason McKrieth, Guard, 2005

Michael Harris, Forward, 2005 (Washington Wizards, Houston Rockets, Utah Jazz)

Brock Gillespie, Guard, 2005

Morris Almond, Guard, 2007 (Utah First Round)

Dolphins in the Pros

Mike Hackett 1982(LA Lakers third round)

Otis Smith 1986 (Denver Nuggets first round)

Danny Pearson 1987 (Washington Bullets seventh round)

Ronnie Murphy 1987 (Portland Trailblazers first round)

Willie McDuffie 1987 (CBA)

Dee Brown 1990 first round (Boston Celtics first round) NBA Slam Dunk Champion

Tim Burroughs 1992 (Minnesota Timberwolves 2nd round)

Willie Fisher 6-8, 1995

Panthers in the Pros

Jay Higginbotham 6-5 Guard 1981

James Harmon 6-7 Forward 1982